Christa McAuliffe
Reaching for the Stars

Patricia Stone Martin

illustrated by Karen Park

Rourke Enterprises Vero Beach, Florida

Manufactured in the United States of America

Library of Congress Cataloging-in-Publication Data

Martin, Patricia Stone.
    Christa McAuliffe –– reaching for the stars.

    (Reaching your goal biographies)
    Summary: Traces the life of the woman selected as the
first teacher-in-space and her tragic death in the
Challenger space shuttle explosion. Includes information
on setting goals.
    1. McAuliffe, Christa, 1948-1986 – Juvenile
literature. 2. Astronauts – United States – Biography
– Juvenile literature. 3. Teachers – New Hampshire –
Biography – Juvenile literature. 4. Challenger
(Spacecraft) – Accidents – Juvenile literature.
[1. McAuliffe, Christa, 1948-1986. 2. Astronauts.
3. Teachers. 4. Challenger (Spacecraft)] I. Title.
II. Series: Martin, Patricia Stone. Reaching your
goal biographies.
TL789.85.M33M37 1987 629.45′0092′4 [B] [92] 87-12902
ISBN 0-86592-172-5

Christa Corrigan stood on a chair. She reached up and pasted a star on the ceiling. Then she looked down at a friend. "I'm reaching for the stars," she said.

The year was 1959, and 11-year-old Christa was in a sixth-grade class for top students. The United States space program was new. It was run by the National Aeronautics and Space Administration (NASA). Christa's class was making a space scene. They hung planets and stars from the ceiling.

Christa stepped down off the chair. She sat by her teacher. Some of her friends sat down too. They talked about being teachers. Eleven years later, Christa did become a teacher. Fifteen years after that, she was chosen to be the first teacher in space.

Sharon Christa McAuliffe was born on September 2, 1948, in Framingham, Massachusetts. Her parents were Edward and Grace Corrigan. She was the oldest of five children.

In high school, Christa dated Steve McAuliffe. After high school she went to Framingham State College. She got a college degree in 1970. That year, Steve and Christa got married.

Christa taught school. She had a baby boy. Steve and Christa named him Scott. Christa earned another degree in 1978 from Bowie State College. Then Christa, Steve, and Scott moved to Concord, New Hampshire. Soon Christa had another baby. It was a girl, and the family named her Caroline.

At first, Christa taught in a junior high school. Then she taught social studies at Concord High School. She taught her students not to be afraid to dream. She said, "Reach for the stars." Sometimes Christa and Steve invited poor children to stay in their home. They wanted to help children.

In 1985, Christa saw her chance to reach for the stars. She heard about the teacher-in-space program. In January she signed up for it. So did over 11,000 other teachers!

That April, Christa was chosen for the program. There were 113 other teachers in the program too. By summer only ten teachers were left in the program. Christa was still one of them.

All ten teachers were sent to the Johnson Space Center in Houston, Texas. They went into training. Every morning they got up at 6:00. They ran on a treadmill. They were put in cloth bags to see if close, dark places bothered them. Each teacher was asked to give a speech. One day the teachers zoomed up and down in a training plane 40 times. They became weightless. They floated in the air. In space people are weightless. Not every one can stand that feeling.

Finally on July 19, 1985, the ten teachers were invited to the White House in Washington, D.C. Only one would be chosen to be the first teacher in space. The first runner-up was named. It was Barbara Morgan. Then the winner was named – Christa McAuliffe!

She was so excited she didn't know what to say. She said, "It's not often a teacher is lost for words." She received a trophy. On the trophy, a child is looking up to a teacher. The teacher is looking up at the stars.

Christa was interviewed on television. The people in Concord held a parade for her. She rode in an open car with her children, Scott and Caroline. Everyone was excited and happy for Christa.

Christa went back into training. An astronaut's training is hard work. Christa learned to do many new things. She also prepared school lessons. She planned to teach two classes from space.

In the lessons, she would tell how it felt to be in space. She would also tell how space looked. A special TV hook-up would carry her lessons back to earth. Children from all over the country would see and hear her.

Long ago pioneer women went west in covered wagons. Christa felt she was like those women. They went to a new place. She was also going to a new place. When she came back, she would tell people about it.

Finally, the day of the lift-off arrived. Christa and the six other astronauts were going to go up in the space shuttle Challenger. They were ready and waiting at the Kennedy Space Center in Florida. But several times NASA scientists stopped the lift-off. Each time something was wrong.

January 28, 1986, was a cold day in Florida. Some people said that the lift-off should not take place that day. They said that the cold weather made the lift-off unsafe. Others said it was safe to go ahead. Finally NASA officials decided to go ahead with the lift-off.

The seven astronauts marched out. Christa was smiling. She gave a thumbs-up sign. Steve, Scott, and Caroline came to Florida to see the lift-off. Caroline was six. Christa's parents and some of her friends were also there.

People were watching the lift-off on TV. Children in classrooms were watching. The boys and girls at Concord High School were excited. They wore party hats. They had noisemakers and streamers ready. Soon one of their teachers would be in space!

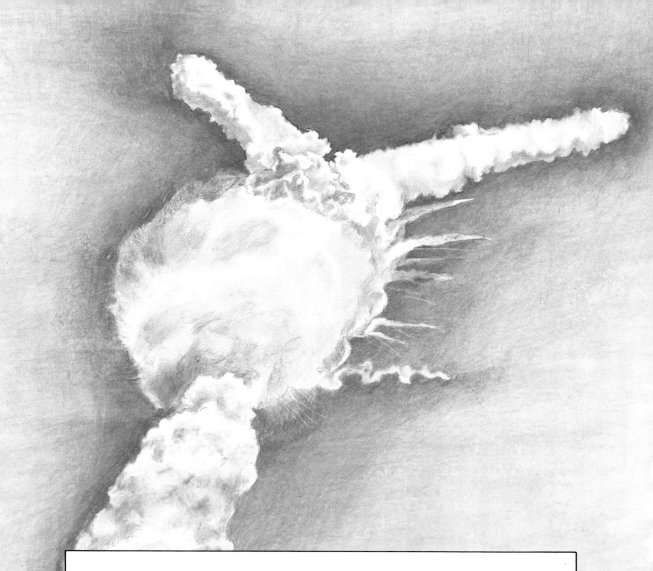

The white space shuttle blasted off. It climbed into the blue sky. Suddenly the shuttle exploded. It made orange and white clouds. Parts of the shuttle went off in different paths through the sky. At first, no one watching could believe what they saw. No one could understand what happened.

Christa and the other astronauts were killed in the explosion. The whole country was sad. But everyone was also proud of their courage. The space program will continue, and someday another teacher will go into space.

Christa told her students, "Whatever it is, try it." She was not afraid. She said, "You can do more than you think you can." Christa McAuliffe reached her goal. She had reached for the stars.

21

Reaching Your Goal

What are your goals? Here are some steps to help you reach them.

1. Decide on your goal.
It may be a short-term goal like one of these:
learning to ride a bike
getting a good grade on a test
keeping your room clean
It may be a long-term goal like one of these:
learning to read
learning to play the piano
becoming a lawyer

2. Decide if your goal is something you really can do.
Do you have the talent you need?
How can you find out? By trying!
Will you need special equipment?
Perhaps you need a piano or ice skates.
How can you get what you need?
Ask your teacher or your parents.

3. Decide on the first thing you must do.
Perhaps this will be to take lessons.

4. Decide on the second thing you must do.
Perhaps this will be to practice every day.

5. Start right away.
Stick to your plan until you reach your goal.

6. Keep telling yourself, "I can do it!"

Good luck! Maybe someday you can be a teacher in space.

Reaching Your Goal Books

Beverly Cleary
She Makes Reading Fun

Bill Cosby Superstar

Jesse Jackson A Rainbow Leader

Ted Kennedy, Jr.
A Lifetime of Challenges

Christa McAuliffe
Reaching for the Stars

Dale Murphy
Baseball's Gentle Giant

Dr. Seuss We Love You

Samantha Smith Young Ambassador

Rourke Enterprises, Inc.
P.O. Box 3328
Vero Beach, FL 32964

GUMDROP BOOKS - Bethany, Missouri